mpliments
Author
Betty Everson.

Coins In A Moonlit Pool

Reflections in verse on many things

Coins In A Moonlit Pool

Reflections in verse on many things

By

Betty Everson

Twilight Gleanings

Date of Publication:
November 1997

Published by :
Twilight Gleanings
Chorley
Lancashire

Printed by:
ProPrint
Riverside Cottage
Great North Road
Stibbington
Peterborough
PE8 6LR

ISBN: 0 9531764 0 1

For every copy sold £1.00 will be
donated to Astley Hall Society,
the 'Friends' who work in support of
Astley Hall

CONTENTS

INTRODUCTION

I have always enjoyed writing poetry. However I do like to spend a lot of time on each poem, revising, polishing and honing the original draft. It is only since I retired that I have had the leisure to do this, without other demands disturbing my concentration.

Although I tend to adhere to the rules of rhyme and metre I learnt many years ago at school (when I first became an enthusiastic poet !)
I sometimes use a free verse style but even so I do like my poems to flow along and not sound stilted. I know I have some old-fashioned ideas about poetry and these are echoed in my title poem, 'Coins in a Moonlit Pool'. I set my standard generally by the great English poets of the past, and do not much care for some of the strange writings that pass for modern 'poetry'!

Everybody seems to be writing these days, and I hesitated considerably before venturing into publishing my own work. However my friends and family appear to enjoy my scribblings and having managed to win a Second Prize in Aural Images 1995 Poetry Competition and had several commendations in other competitions I feel I cannot be too bad a poet and that a wider audience might gain some pleasure from this little collection.

Being a linguist, I have been influenced by poetry in languages other than English and it was a French poem* which inspired 'The Poet's Medium' which won me my prize. 'Spell', 'Silence', 'Grand-daughter', 'The Jugoslav Seaman' and 'To an Elizabethan Lady' have all been variously commended. The last-named reflects my involvement with Astley Hall Society and its historical costumes as do 'Astley Hall' and 'Cromwell's Boots'.

I have included three early poems (1950-70) 'The Beacons', 'Ebbtide' and 'Inspiration' but the rest have been written over the last ten years and several have appeared in general anthologies.

* Théophile Gautier: 'L'Art'

ACKNOWLEDGEMENT

I should like to thank my family and friends for their encouraging comments on my work but my especial thanks go to my husband, Derrick, who has patiently read many first drafts of my poems and whose constructive criticism has inspired me to ever greater efforts.

DEDICATION

In memory of my parents, with love, and with gratitude.

COINS IN A MOONLIT POOL

Come not too close with your analysis
Of words that burst and bubble on the page;
Think not here lies some soul-evoked catharsis
In lines that sing or bleakly roar and rage.

My poems are but random thoughts, ideas
That probing coax my unskilled hand to tool
These fleeting images of joy and tears;
Toss them as coins, deep in a moonlit pool.

Remote as dreams beneath the mirrored wake
Of clouds that flirt with silver-shafting moon
They glint distorted where night-breezes rake
The water's face, then through stirred ripples swoon.

Half-won philosophies abandoned lie
Obscure in weed-enshrouded depths below;
Through shadowed branches laughing fairies spy
With mocking eyes on each flawed cameo.

They fall far short , those puny verses cast
Into the pool, of visions that inspire
And yet elude my pen; fickle at last,
My teasing muse snuffs out the kindled fire.

Like bards of old I would have made my mark,
My poems heard acclaimed with loud drum-roll,
But now they slide into that glimmering dark,
Coins disregarded in a moonlit pool.

THE POET'S MEDIUM

How shall we depict save with black words
The images our straining minds design?
There is no rainbow wash
To brush with vibrant strokes across the page,
And brittle words we cannot mould
As yielding clay at teasing finger's, touch;
Yet words may etch a tracery to match
The print of sunlight shafting through veined leaves,
Or flash bright patterns, fleet as mirrored fire
Of crystals frozen in eternal snow.

How shall we chant the soul's bleak cry
Or melodise triumphant exultation?
Here are no velvet tones of violoncello
Nor winsome trilling of the flute,
No roll of drums, nor trumpet's victory call;
The only cadences we have are words
Which with musician's skill we must attune
And fashion to compelling plaint
Or far-resounding hymn of joy.

How shall we wrest from tumbling, random thoughts
The essence of conceived philosophy
As pungent oils encapsulate
The fleeting fragrances of summer flowers?
Only in the subjuguation
Of crowding, clamouring words,
And banishment of every superfluity,
Shall lie revealed splendid upon the page
The distillation of our dreamings.

A DAY IN THE LIFE OF A GRANNY

I'm staying with Peter and life is all go!
First thing in the morning, it's 'Up, Granny! NOW!'
Thomas Tank Engine's waiting with Gordon and James,
And all of my cars; we can play lots of games!

I'll be the Policeman and Postman Pat,
The Bus Driver in my bus driver's hat,
The man at the garage and Fireman Sam,
And you're the Mummy, with Baby in a pram!

'I'm tired of all that; now, let's make a farm!
No, no, Granny, that's not the place for the barn!
Put it here, by the stable; look, here's the horse;
The sheep and cows go in the field, *of course*!'

Lunch-time at last! Then, 'Come and sit beside me!
We can watch Playbus while you drink your coffee;
And then Mummy's video'd 'Sesame Street' ';
And straight after that I'm back on my feet!

Peter's off to the park for a pedal-bike ride;
Then he has an idea: he'll walk *up* the slide!
Roundabout, swings, see-saw: he just can't stop,
'Look at me on the climbing-frame, right at the top!'

Home again;   'What can we do after tea?
You could read one of my books to me;
Those are my crayons, perhaps we could draw!
I know! Shall we do my new jigsaw?'

And now, at last it's time for bed,
Up we go for a bath with Tigger and Ted;
'Good-night, Granny! I do love you!
To-morrow, shall we make a zoo?'

GRAND-DAUGHTER

I croon a lullaby that links
The generations
Over the newborn princess in my arms;
Two eyes darkly blue gaze up at me, questioning,
With her father's frown,
My right to clasp her close.

Purposefully against my tiring heart
The tiny body pulsates,
Each new-drawn breath a confirmation
Of life's renewal;
The sturdy limbs stretch and kick.
Proclaiming the fount
Of a life-time's energy;
Dainty fists flail the air
In eager quest and burgeoning awareness,
Until with hungry wail
The pretty mouth is opened wide
In cavernous dimension,
Setting pink tongue and toothless gums a quiver,
And her face, distorted,
Forfeits awhile its promised beauty.

Smiling I rise,
Wincing at arthritic twinge,
And surrender my grand-daughter
To her mother's breast.

My little girl; how may I express the joy,
The awe of holding you,
To know the cycle now begins again
In you, the heiress to a thousand dreams,
Triumphs, injustice, pain,
Such as women for centuries have known?
In wonderment I cede my place to you,
As the withered bloom,
Casting its faded petals on the air,
Yields to the bud new-sprung upon the stem.

TO AN ELIZABETHAN LADY

I saw you there by oaken panelling
When evening's dying rays through casement fell
And set your silver kirtle glistening
Like summer rain in darkening forest dell.

Your gown of green wide-flared on farthingale
Half-merged with shadows, sleeve's distended puff
Slashed to reveal white shift, a partlett pale
Laid modestly beneath the snowy ruff.

A meshed pomander on long chain of gold
Hung from the girdle clasped about your waist;
The French hood with pearl billiments soft-scrolled
Your wistful features poignantly embraced.

Your presence faded as last shafting beam
Withdrew its light: then, were you ghost or dream?

ASTLEY HALL

Beside the lake in Astley Park the Hall
Serenely stands, by distant heir bestowed
On Chorley folk, with treasures to enthral,
And tales to charm, of ancestral abode.

The path of English history here is traced:
Plots Catholic against Elizabeth,
Priest's hole and secret Mass, Charnocks disgraced,
With Babington John cruelly put to death.

As if at birthing, from the caryatid
In Morning Room Sir Robert's features spy,
While dolphins leap, with tulips strangely paired,
And ancient myths in ceiling sculptured lie.

A Royalist Captain's portrait, 'One-eye' named,
Who gallantly at Lathom House once fought,
Bespeaks enigma, for nearby high-framed
The Lord Protector's likeness gives us thought.

The oaken mouldings on his bed impose
Yet grace no longer Cromwell's Room, forsooth!
So did the Roundhead seeking night's repose
Leave here his boots? Who knows the truth?

An heiress' marriage now they celebrate;
In Restoration splendour themes baroque
Spill from the plastered ceilings, dominate
The Hall new-fashioned of Sir Peter Brooke.

A century passes; evening sunlight slants
Through diamond panes across Long Gallery;
On Shovel-board the coloured patterns dance
As counters tossed in bygone rivalry.

Susannah blessed with this inheritance
Weds Thomas Townley-Parker; newly flowers
Their cherished home in Georgian elegance;
The son with Astley widowed mother dowers.

For Robert now at Cuerden will reside;
Childless his heir, yet Astley will outlast
The fading lineage: our benefactor's pride
Exhorts us to preserve its glories past.

Charnocks, Brooks, Townley-Parkers, all are gone;
Our heritage at Astley Hall lives on!

CROMWELL'S BOOTS

On through the pelting rain the Ironsides sped
With victory flushed, athirst for Royalist blood;
Across the sodden fields the Scots horde fled
And men and horses cursed the squelching mud.

'A deluge such as this I ne'er have known,'
Quoth mighty Cromwell as the black night fell,
We'll here make camp for to the very bone
This rain doth penetrate. I once heard tell
That on this dismal land amongst the trees
Lies Astley Hall; night's shelter there I'll seek,
God's truth! with Royalist Charnock take my ease,
Of Lathom House with its defender speak.'

The Hall in that wet darkness silent stood
As Robert fast in nightmare frenzy trapped
Heard once again the cannon-ball's near thud,
His hand to eyeless socket groaning clapped;
And still the rain poured down in ceaseless stream,
Wind-driven rattled at the window-pane,
Pounding like fists into tormented dream.
At Robert's side wife Alice restless lain,
Started from fitful sleep as through the storm
Broke sounds of horses, troopers' stealthy tramp.
In fear she cried: 'Are then the Roundheads come?'
'Nay, sleep again; they do but make their camp;
Their clamour with the dawn we'll hear no more
For Hamilton they'll down to Wigan hound.'
There came a thundering at the oaken door,
And Alice screamed while Robert at one bound
Was breeched, then sword in hand downstairs he came.
White-faced his steward hastened to his side.
'Open, ye Royalist dogs in Cromwell's name!'
The bolts were drawn; 'Ho, Charnock! Here I'll bide!

Thou one-eyed rogue! Is't not a goodly jest?
The siege at Lathom House cost half thy sight
When me thou didst defy, yet now, thy weary guest,
I'll lie beneath thy roof on this foul night!
Thy kinsman, Stephen, tutor to my son,
A godly man for all thy heresy,
Leads us to truce; no mischief shall be done,
Nor vengeance wreaked upon thy family,
At daybreak I'll be gone; is't not well said?
Come, Madam, maids, cast off those looks forlorn!
Fetch me hot water, linen for my bed!
Take these my boots; they must be dry by morn!'

With such a scurry, flurry now they ran,
The Roundhead General's bidding to perform,
Bustling with candles, jugs and warming-pan
Like bees in hive disturbed, a frantic swarm.

Sleepless the household lay till morning broke;
With noisy shouts and curses Cromwell rose
To find his boots still wet. In wrath he spoke:
'Give me another pair! Whose boots are those?'
'The master's sir!' replied a trembling youth;
'In truth, they're neatly made, well-soled and heeled!
Why, Charnock's boots I'll wear this day, forsooth!
They'll serve me well on yonder battlefield!'

Then, should you ever go to Astley Hall,
Look to the glass-case where in proud display
Two ancient leather boots do yet recall
That rainy night when Cromwell passed this way!

CHILDHOOD SUMMER

And now it seems a century ago
I woke to doves roo-cooing in the dawn,
To restive horses whinnying below
As early footfall sang on cobblestone.

My Pegasus bestrode the downland turf
Where rabbits fled to chalky burrow's floor;
The rising sun illumed the pearly surf
Of distant combers raking pebbled shore.

Morn-gathered mushrooms sizzled in the pan,
Their fragrance wafting, torment of delight!
In globuled juices velvet-lush they swam,
A morning feast on plates of gleaming white.

Then to the sea with swim-suit, pail and spade,
Into the gentle swell, with headlong splash
Exultant swimmers plunged to crests of jade
While timid paddlers trailed at water's edge.

Spread-eagled on the beach with hunger stilled
We watched the ebbing tide, the wheeling gulls
Till new shore treasures lured where winkles spilled
From green-slimed rocks upturned in myriad pools.

Proud moated castles fashioned in the sand
Stood vulnerable to evening cricket-game
As drugged with salty air our bodies tanned
Ran, gilded silhouettes in sunset flame.

Home now, as rising breezes stirred
And sandy footprints left their lingering mark
Along the hedgerowed lanes as first nightbird
Trilled, harbinger of honeysuckled dark.

AUTUMN PAST

The autumn of childhood: when woodlands blazed
With burnish of copper and bronze and gold
And windows by Jack Frost's fingers were glazed
Is a time I remember now I am old.

A time when we gathered pears, apples and plums,
Made jam, pickle, chutney, sought nuts in the lanes,
When robins on doorstep stood looking for crumbs
And swallows took flight with the first chill rains;

When we helped make Christmas puddings and cake,
Dug up potatoes, stacked logs in the shed,
Fearful of witch's spell lay wide awake
On Hallowe'en night in warm feather-bed;

When the cold winds blew and with rake and broom
We swept up dead leaves as they round our feet whirled,
Then tramped in to tea in a gas-lit room
As smoke from the smouldering bonfire curled;

When the stark silhouette of bare-branched trees
Blackly etched against sunset sky foretold
The sharp frosts heralding winter freeze,
That's a time I remember now I am old.

THE MEADOW

Meadowsweet,
Encapsulating memories
Of summer's fragrant days,
Of carefree childhood spent
In meadow, sweet with daisies, buttercups
And meadowsweet.

The silken wings of butterfly
Atop a flaxen head
Vied shimmering with dragonfly and moth,
While Grandad vigilant stood by
To watch and guide
And wrestle with the gate
Which led into the meadow,
Where the grass grew
Unmolested
Beneath a sun that blazed forever,
So it seemed,
And made the meadow bright
With blue-starred cornflowers,
Poppies poster-red;
And all the sound we knew
Was song of birds,
Of lark and thrush and chattering jay,
Or hum of insect,
Pollen-questing bee and restless wasp,
Save for the chugging engine
Leaving its trail of vapour
Rounded, rhythmically puffed,
Till lost in following the distant slope
To nothingness,
Beyond the daisies, buttercups
And meadowsweet.

Meadow sweet with cherry blossom
Holding captive juice,
At autumn's call in rebel springs to rise
And stain the pie-dish rim,
With petalled pastry clasped about,
And glisten purple as an Emperor's cloak.

Meadow sweet with pink-foamed apple-trees
Bent low, soon sturdily to bear
Their summer burden,
Sweet ripened fruits to store red-gold
In woodshed, barn,
Or pungently define
High-raftered loft,
Each in its dimpled place by gnarled hand laid
As tenderly as babe in cradling down.

Childhood was sweet,
A drift of fleeting blossom,
Vanishing as dream in dawn's first mists,
Your passing bitter-sweet,
For winter rides the gate
And summer's smiling promise is betrayed;
Disillusion
Clouds the golden day
As coarse bricks and concrete choke
The meadow grass,
And banished now are all the daisies, buttercups
And meadowsweet.

MEMORIES OF HOMESICK MOOD IN AUSTRIA

Oh, for a glimpse of wind-raked Yorkshire moor
Benignly sheltering on valley floor
The busy town with chimneys tall below,
Time-blackened mills and houses row on row;
Glass roof of workroom lit by noonday sun
Flashing through smoky haze where wool is spun,
And moorland beck swollen by summer rain
Girdling the dark stone walls like silver chain.

A swing-bridge opens passage on canal,
The barges chug, the squawk of waterfowl
Echoes across the purple-heathered steeps
Where pagan altar stony vigil keeps,
The shepherd's collie zealously zigzags
To gather errant sheep from rocky crags,
As sunset glowing gilds their dingy fleece
And bathes the air around with roseate peace.

Or southwards where the primroses yet bloom
In joyful clusters down the shady combe
And harebells frail in sea-borne summer breeze
Nod on the downland turf, and chalk-falls tease
The scurrying rabbits, bobtails flashing white
While seagulls toss and weave in restless flight;
And far below in cornfields rippling gold
The poppies scarlet in the sun unfold.

See how the gardens washed by fleeting shower,
Are bright again with every summer flower:
Lupin, delphinium and sunflower tall,
Rose, hollihock, sweet pea on sunny wall;
A cricket match with figures white on green,
The click of bat on ball, my English scene,
While on the shore the children watch sad-eyed
Sandcastles crumbling with the evening tide.

The hills enfold the valleys north and south;
Gentle their slopes, these alien giants uncouth
Tower dizzyingly above the narrow dales
And hide their snow-capped heads in cloudy veils;
In darkening skies forked lightning earthward streaks
And crashing thunder rolls about the peaks
Till at storm's passing sunset briefly flares
And yields too hastily to rising stars:
Give me those skies of amethyst and rose
Caressing England's fells at daylight's close.

PARIS REVISITED

We are two old ladies now,
Making our unsteady way along the boulevards,
Jostled by the young, heedless, unaware
Of the nostalgia which makes us smile:
'Tu te rappelles? Do you remember? '

.....Paris reawakening in the post-war years
When we were young and walked,
Click-click on our high heels,
Down the Champs-Elysées, Rue de Rivoli,
Across the Place de la Concorde, pausing
In the Tuileries Gardens to drink tea with lemon,
Then running for the bus,
Precariously,
Click-click on our high heels,
Laughing, clinging to each other
On the platform as it swayed,
A glimpse of sunset gilding the Sacré-Coeur.

Without fear walking the streets by night,
Strangely diffused lamplight casting
Monster puppet images over derelict bomb-sites,
The Moulin Rouge turning starkly under the stars;

On Bastille night dancing till dawn
In streets burgeoning with overcrowded cafés,
Celebrating an ancient Revolution,
Drinking to the ending of a World War.
The mood was upbeat. We were alive.....

..... Sophisticated illumination to-night bejewels
The Eiffel Tower, the Arc de Triomphe, Notre-Dame:
Sadly we gaze from car-window on the nocturnal façade,
Two old ladies, fearing the peace-spawned terrors
Lurking in the streets of our youth.

EBBTIDE

What then am I doing, here upon the shore,
Sad farewells still echoing, telling the breakers' roar,
Dreams of mountains fading as the sullen waters pound,
Wail to the mind dejected, in caverns tranced resound?

What then am I doing, here upon the hill,
Watching the silent vista, seeing the billows spill,
Flash in the glinting sunlight, vanish in vaporous swirl,
Leaving the pain to slumber, oblivion's flags unfurl?

What now am I doing, here beneath the trees,
Lost in this tender autumn, hearing the sobbing seas?
Spring's green torment is ended, lethargy claims the day,
The future waits unbidden, a step, a winter away.

TO MY MIRROR, ON GROWING OLD

Mirror, you surely lie? That's none of me!
Those dulling, red-rimmed eyes, late pools of green
Reflecting laughter, girlish reverie,
And all the hopes and fears of sweet eighteen.

Mirror, you merciless make mocking play
Of furrowed lines that tell me I am old,
Of sparse hair yielding to encroaching grey:
Where now's the rosy bloom, the tumbling gold?

O wicked looking-glass, so to distort
The once-trim figure with unseemly girth;
The mind still agile brims with teeming thought,
Gives voice to passion, anger, tears and mirth.

Cruel mirror, imaging the time-worn shell,
Will you not show the inner me as well ?

GEM-FANTASY

A sapphire ringed about with pebbles cool
Its gleam at twilight yields in dark rock-pool;
Here waves lie harnessed till the new tide's flow,
The polished water mirrors starlit glow:
Reach out your hand and pluck now from the night
The pendant moonstone, clasp its pallid light:
So madness in your palm has left its sting,
Beware unearthly laughter echoing
In vaulted hall and on the turret-stair;
Beware the phantom's curse, the werewolf's lair!

In dreary mine, as ancient legends deep,
Seam-bound the priceless brilliants glint and keep
Their watchful vigil in the dusty shaft;
The toiling pitman plies his clumsy craft
Till, mounting from the cavern's man-torn scars,
He glimpses heaven in a million stars;
As skywards, tranced, his rolling eye-whites turn
And planet-diamonds bright the pupils burn,
With pick-axe would he cleave the heaving sky,
Prise out the stars embedded where they lie.

Eastwards the morning breezes, bustling, lean,
The matted cloudbanks tease to nacrous sheen,;
Uncurling coral fingers gently probe
And goad to wakefulness the sleeping globe:
Have you on drowsy pillow lain at dawn
In blissful torpor, curtains semi-drawn,
Through lazy lids to watch the brimming blue
While trilling song-birds call to waken you?
Their measures with the dazzling azure vie,
Lapis lazuli, morning lullaby .....
With hey ! and ho ! you open wide your eyes;
At last, with cat-like dalliance you rise
To see the dew-borne emeralds on the grass,
Quartz-lamps a-flicker as the sun-darts pass.

Where brightest topaz dances on the sea
With sober jade in chequered harmony,
Frail crystal horses leap from out the foam
As with the noonday flames the amber dome,
Casting its beams across the arid land
And searing deck-chair sleepers on the sand.

The slanting rays slip through the latticed pane
And garnets ripple in the polished grain
Of cabinet, bright-shone mahogany;
Great-grandma peeps at curtain-lace to see
The cherry-rubies on the black tree-bough;
With pearl-brooch toying she remembers how
The rosy jewels flashed in candle-light
When Lady Beatrice entertained that night
Her secret lover; how in haste returned
Lord Archibald, by secret word forewarned;
'He strode right up, his lordship, to Jack's side
And shot him where he sat, and there he died;
He shot her too; her gown was soaked in blood,
Red as those rubies; they did her no good!'

The bloodstone flickers red, then fades from view
As amethyst enfolds each dying hue;
Day casts its tattered dreams on sunset pyre,
To-morrow's hopes are forged in opal's fire;
The burnished shadows cede in misting scene,
Their lustre spent, to star-pricked tourmaline.

THE BEACONS (LES PHARES)

Is there a light ahead,
A light in the future?
Are there no beacons
To flash down the coast,
To flash down the line
From the past to the future,
Is there no promise
Of harbour ahead?

Cast on life's ocean,
Drifting, unanchored,
The past far behind,
In the darkness, untraced,
The future a pace away
Veiled to our vision,
This Moment, our Present,
We hold, this our Life.

No messenger speeds
From the past to the future,
The voice of proud eras
Is silent, unknown
To those in the shadowbound
Ages awaiting
Their moment of Pageant,
Their Passing , their Time.

Each one of us cries
From the ocean about us,
Is there no hope,
No relief from our pain?
And all the lost ages
Are silent about us,
No message for us
From the prisons of Time.

THE LIGHTHOUSE

At dusk the lighthouse on the headland wakes
And distant mountains yield to purple gloom;
The dazzling gleam through deepening shadows breaks,
A golden flower of night in its first bloom.

On quay and hillside burgeoning lamps respond
And wink their greeting to the pulsing light
As rising mists with floral hues abscond
And white-washed houses hide in mantling night.

Jewel-bright like necklaces along the shore
The lanterns sway; their images below
In dimpling swathes across the water's floor
Flirt with the shafting signal's mirrored glow.

Now pebble castanets their beat intone
While dancing foam-flecked breakers swish and swirl,
And at tide's edge, with sparkling brilliants sewn,
The lacy hems of eddying flounces whirl.

The ribboned moonlight trips on silken waves;
Flamenco music haunts the lover's dream
As probing rocky clefts and hidden caves
The beacon flares with mesmerising beam.

DAWN

(An attempt at a poem in Villanelle Form)

Darkness fades, steals in the morrow,
Day-sound breaking stirs nightly hush,
Wakens blackbird, lark and swallow.

Shadows yield in vale and hollow,
Widening sun-rays forests brush,
Darkness fades, steals in the morrow.

Pennant-mists entwine green willow,
Dew-drop gleams in lakeside bulrush,
Wakens blackbird, lark and swallow.

Childhood stirs on dream-steeped pillow,
Youth the rebel flees dawn's ambush,
Darkness fades, steals in the morrow.

Loudly twitters chirpy sparrow,
Vies with sleepy call of song-thrush,
Wakens blackbird, lark and swallow.

Redgold glow fires townhouse window,
Glistens on tarmac's mirrored flush,
Darkness fades, steals in the morrow,
Wakens blackbird, lark and swallow.

TO NANCY

A brown leaf falling brushed my cheek
As once your dying brushed my heart;
You stood on winter's threshold bleak;
Too soon its chill drew us apart.

The seeds of death already sown,
In your frail frame grew unrestrained,
Yet in your eyes the laughter shone,
Made protest as life's vigour waned.

My mind reached out to yours; your gaze
Held fast my own: at once I knew
The task which lately filled your days
In silent pledge I must pursue.

You drooped before me like a leaf
Which once had danced green in the sun,
Then gleamed in golden splendour brief
Till withered brown its life was done.

Farewell, dear friend; would we had met
Ere autumn cast its ragged cloak;
On misty air sighs sweet regret
As tumbling leaves pale ghosts evoke.

WRITTEN ON HEARING OF THE DEATH OF JOHN SMITH, LEADER OF THE LABOUR PARTY 12TH MAY 1994

When John Smith died in that stark, tragic dawn,
There came a memory of a summer storm,
Of crashing thunder, lightning flashing close,
Of spark and flame, of regal standard rose
With severed bush brought down, a lifeless form.

So was the Red Rose from the proud branch torn,
As fateful lightning struck the tree new-grown;
Across the sky the black clouds serried lour:
With senses numbed we mourn in darkest hour
That such a man came not into his own.

This was a man who spoke with prophet's ire,
Whose vision burned, unquenchable his fire,
A man of true compassion, one who cared
That degradation, poverty ensnared,
Held fast his fellows in despair's black mire.

A man whom rank injustice so concerned,
Who on its perpetrators his wrath turned,
Who rose above the petty bickering,
The mocking ploy of filibustering,
With ready wit and humour critics spurned.

There on near-conquered peak we saw him stand:
A dying Leader glimpsed the Promised Land;
A New Dawn breaks as probes first shafting ray
Through the dark clouds and lights once more the way
He sought to follow, where yet points his hand.

THE JUGOSLAV SEAMAN

We took your photograph in that last year
Of blue-skied peace on Adriatic shore;
There was no thought of strife, no hint of fear:
We did not dream we should come back no more.

You painted your old boat in green and white,
And laughed with us because the day was fair;
We did not speak your tongue, yet our delight
Was one with yours in fragrant summer air.

Your deep-set eyes still gaze on us to-day,
Half-shaded by the cap you smiling raised;
The quayside scene in breeze-kissed sunlight's play
Bespeaks an idyll by war's hand erased.

Where are you now, old seaman Mario?
Did you take flight to distant mountain-steep
As gunfire raked the harbour wall below?
Or do you cowering in bombed hovel weep?

Did you set sail in your new-painted boat
And reach a land where exiled now you grieve?
Or did you choose to fight, defend that spot
Which blithe we shared with you on conflict's eve?

And do you lie by sniper's bullet felled
Amidst the carnage, in last pose obscene?
This memory yet is in our album held:
'Mario paints his boat in white and green'

TRAVELLING GRANNIES

You must have seen them; they're legion , the Grannies,
Clutching their holdalls and weekend cases,
Travelling with railcards on Supersaver,
Helping to keep British Rail ticking over,
Going to welcome a new little one
And say to the siblings, 'Haven't you grown !'

Their seats are booked on Intercity
And they settle down with 'Woman's Weekly',
Or knit away at a bobble-topped hat,
A pullover blazoned with Postman Pat;
More erudite Grannies tackle a crossword,
Browse through 'The Times', reminisce about Oxford.

Then out come the lunch-boxes, thermos flasks steam;
The buffet's too dear, or too far, it would seem,
To reach through a swaying procession
Of carriages, though some venture down
For sandwiches, coffee or, with a smile,
'A G. and T., please; let's travel in style!'

They know where to change at the main line stations,
Which platforms to head for to catch their connections:
Under the subway and over the footbridge,
Dodging the crowds, avoiding the scrimmage,
And if there is time, grab a quick cup of tea:
'I daren't miss the train; they'll be waiting for me!'

The journey's been long, but here's the last lap;
Tiredness marks faces, lids droop to a nap
In the comforting warmth of suburban train;
The slow minutes pass in the soothing refrain
Of wheels rattling onwards, station by station,
Carrying them to their destination
They look out for daughters waiting to meet them;
Then toddling down the platform to greet them
The grandchildren come: 'There's Granny!' they call;
Surely you've seen them, those loved Grannies all?

IN PRAISE OF OSTEOPATHY

'There's an ache in my left shoulder
And a tingling in my arm,'
'A strained muscle,' said my doctor;
'Use this salve and keep it warm!'

A few weeks later dizzy spells
Called for a new prescription:
'Three times a day, now, take these pills;
You've got water retention!'

But things got worse; 'Slow down your pace,'
A new G.P. advised me;
'Old age brings trials you'll have to face!'
And I had just turned fifty!?

The world was spinning round and round,
The pain was diabolical;
In dull despair my teeth I ground,
I was feeling suicidal!

'You really can't go on like this,'
Said a friend who crossed my path,
'You need a new diagnosis!
Why not try my osteopath?'

The osteopath was very kind,
'Pain, tingling? Lost your verve?'
The symptoms she had soon defined:
'Vertigo?   You've trapped a nerve!'

'Now here's the source of your distress!'
I heard a kind of click!
'We'll need more time to treat this mess;
Can you come back next week?'

Yes!..... and the next!.... And then again
When osteo-arthritis plagued me,
A prolapsed disc, all kinds of pain:
Three cheers for osteopathy!

SILENCE

How vibrant those moments!
No harsh sound intrusive
Jarred senses; I relive,
In mind yet held captive,
The memory of silence:

The silence of ravine:
Clear water moving,
Through rock-face grooving,
Sun-fingers delving
Where moss glistens green.

The silence of rainbow:
Over cliff projecting
Rain-washed light, reflecting
Swathed hues diffracting
In sea-spray below.

The silence of cottage;
Cloud shadows racing,
Dark wall embracing,
In moonlight tracing
Patterns in whitewash.

The silence of snowfall:
Bridal veil gliding,
Swirl on swirl sliding,
Crude blemish hiding
In white sculpted crystal.

How treasured those moments
Of ravine and rainbow,
Cottage and fall of snow;
Beacon-bright still they glow,
Rare islands of silence.

INSPIRATION

Perplexed my mind,
Staring the black confusion of notes
Amassed across thin green-blue.

Then, like the first trickle
Of the river's source
A fleeting idea jabs at that armoury
Of fruitless reflection,
Splashing into the toiling recesses
Of my mind
Which absorbs it with furtive hesitation,
Afraid of the cessation of the brief flow;
But, following the first venturesome drop,
Another bubbles forth,
Chasing its brother,
And a third
And another,
Larger and faster they flow
Till they teem in rich cascades,
Now seething, now dragging at each other
In torrential fall,
And now in quieter pools
The undercurrents pull, and at last
Succumb to the main stream
Which like a mighty river
Drifts onward to fulfilment.

My pen writes on;
The sudden flight of thoughts
Guides its movement,
For my hand has lost control
Of this strange weapon of my mind;
The steady flow of fountain blue
Curves and shapes itself
Until my quivering brain, oppressed
By this impersonal flood,
Calls a halt, in sudden doubt of its power,
And the magic moment is past.

SPELL

Give me a little wizardry,
For I would transfix
That moment when the dusk is poised
To drape its cloak of grey
About my garden;
That moment when the last frail streak
Of amethyst holds night at bay
And Venus rising pricks the purple sky,
When disembodied moon-flowers gleam
And latent colours haunt
The sleepy eye,
When burnished silhouettes of bush and tree
Linger in shadow's wake.

That moment when the air still redolent
With scent of rose and lavender and thyme
Is newly-laced
With herald fragrances of night,
Elusive honeysuckle, sweet geranium,
And nightingale first trills
The evening incantation.

That moment when on distant coast
A beacon glimmers, stirs
Half-doubted, half-perceived;
When fishing-boats,
Passing through spectral harbour-mouth,
Are not quite one
With sea and sky,
And glow-worm lanterns
On slow-dancing ships
Flit
Now near, now far,
Over white-flecked waters.

BIRDSONG ON NEW YEAR'S EVE

When I reflect now on a new beginning
As the Old Year ends and the New Year's winging
On the joyous bells whirling in distant spire,
And the remnants of festive cheer new inspire
With bright resolve hearts in rose-hued dimension,
Filled with season's goodwill and brave intention,
I recall how I stood alone at midnight
By a frosted window pale-brushed by starlight
And heard in the shrubbery darkly spilling
The song of a nightbird's delicate trilling;
As I listened entranced my confused thoughts fled;
Those projects and plans chasing round in my head
Blurred, faded, dissolved on that quiet New Year's Eve
And my thoughts to-day to that rare idyll cleave.

So over the years when the peal comes tumbling
With soul-piercing chime, and once more we're fumbling
At which resolution to make for this year,
Wakes the memory of birdsong echoing clear;
Those pure, fragile notes seem to draw me apart
From the frivolous scene; intone in my heart
A maxim to follow in all that I do;
Hold fast through the year to the things that are true.

THE SWANS AT MARTIN MERE

Soaring to frost-bound altitudes unborned,
Their broad-spanned pinions riding air-stream's play,
The swans have flown two thousand fearless miles,
Taut throats outstretched, eyes scanning star-set way.

I half-mistook strange bugling in the dawn
For trumpet-blast of angel-heralds near;
Yet this was but their joyful carolling
At journey's ending, high above the mere.

In circling patterns sliding down the sky,
Their forms take shape, then bird by bird swoop low
To ruffled water, where in classic pose
They fold their wings, curve necks to supple bow.

As darkness falls and sleepy water-fowl
Make fractious murmur in the chilly night,
The swans serenely glide on floodlit lake,
Their regal plumage gleaming waxy-white.

Late homing birds descend with rush of wings,
Evoking fantasies in spellbound eyes
Of downy chariots drawn by soft-plumed steeds
Or Zeus to Leda come in feathered guise.

Once more by day now mesmerised we stand
And watch the wintering migrants' wheeling flight;
Bright-mirrored sky in ribboned water glints
On distant wetlands brushed by shafting light.

As shadows this tranquillity embrace
From hide we cast a lingering glance to where,
In dying sunset fire etched amethyst,
The swans hold court again at Martin Mere.

SEASCAPE

The boom of the surf on the cold shore breaking,
The hiss of the undertow, pebbles raking,
The whisper of spray on the wave-crest waking:
Tidal symphony, music of the sea.

The gleam of the white-winged gull steep wheeling,
The flash of gold from the lighthouse stealing,
Fitful clouds round the headland reeling:
Cliff-top gallery, pictures of the sea.

The tang of seaweed in ship's wake shifting,
The smell of fish from the dockside drifting,
The waft of tar through the beached nets sifting;
Lure of the senses, opiates of the sea.

The bark of the seal at day's end mourning,
The scream of the kittiwake, predators warning,
The laugh of the dolphin, slow ships scorning:
Wind-borne incantations, spells of the sea.

Startled crab out of harm's way gliding,
Mussel and winkle in rock-pool hiding,
Wispy prawns through the soft sand sliding:
Bucket, spade and shrimp-net, childhood by the sea.

Desert islands, pirate-ships, mermaids singing,
Smuggler in cavern dark, lantern swinging,
Sunken city with ghost-bell ringing:
Old sea-dog's treasury, yarns of the sea.

Galleon treasure-laden, homeward racing,
Through new-charted oceans passage tracing,
Eastern spices the breezes lacing:
Merchant and mariner, home from the sea.

Ice-bergs and coral reefs, hurricanes blowing,
Tempests and sea-mists, beacons glowing,
Sandbanks and rocky straits, cross-currents flowing:
Echoes at new tide the call of the sea.

THE RIVER

Here where the muddy riverbed
Near-drained of water lies exposed,
Where drought has struck, the wildfowl fled,
Where rusty bike and old pram tossed
Lurk in foul slime, obscene displays,
Was where we spent our summer days.

Here where the frogs no longer spring
From grassy bank or stony ledge
We fished with jam-jars on a string
For sticklebacks at water's edge,
Played ducks and drakes, sailed home-made boats,
Or channelled water for castle-moats.

Just down the road was this paradise
Where, sharing a bottle of lemonade,
We paddled beneath unpolluted skies,
Watched kingfishers dive in willow's shade,
Then sat on the bridge, feet dangling low,
And peered at our images mirrored below.

We could go there in safety; never a car
Disturbed the peace of our childhood dream;
Mothers knew no qualms as we wandered far
On the paths that followed our sparkling stream;
There was none to harm the child who chased
Bright butterflies, or larks' flight traced.

But now on busy tarmac road,
Jostling, traffic's endless scrimmage
Roars over joyless riverbed
Where once the lane and wooden bridge
Echoed to children's footsteps bound
For river-haunt, our lost playground.

THE RAINBOW

The rainbow spans the lane,
Arching eastwards
Over farm and field,
Brushing with misting hues
The fleece of sheep;
Reaching westward beyond
The grassy edge of cliff to where
The colours dip,
Caress the marbled sea,
Diffract
In diamond-studded spray.

The rainbow blooms and blossoms
As if the Gardener, striding across the sky
Has planted, row on row, red roses, marigolds
And golden rod entangling summer ferns,
With bright delphiniums and gentian
To border heather sprays.

Or the Draper,
Through shop-window glimpsed,
As bursting sun-beams probe the dusty gloom,
With salesman's pride
The vibrant swathes unfurls
To toss their glory down the counter's length.

The garden fades,
The shop is lost to view;
Bereft of sparkle
Cold the rain-drops fall
Upon the sheep,
Become grey statues in their field,
And on the sea darkly racing
Towards the shore.

SOPHIE

Born under Leo, so always the boss,
Our remarkably beautiful Collie-cross
Is as arrogant as her Belgian mum,
But loving us yields when we say 'Come!'

Dainty as colt, her feet scarce touch the ground,
Though if on the lead for the woods she's bound
She bumbles along like a hulking bear,
Ears twitching, nose probing, scenting the air
For scurrying rabbits she soon will chase;
Fleet as a cheetah, with roe-deer's grace,
A bronze streak, she leaps through the autumn ferns,
Head flickering black, throat white as she turns.

With banner-tail waving she hastens home;
Her food will be ready, perhaps a bone
Which with wolfish glee she'll begin to gnaw
Till, ever alert, she hears the fridge door;
Foxy-sly sidles in my kitchen maid:
For a fallen crumb her soul she'd trade!

As daylight fades and curtains are drawn
She flops on the carpet with a yawn,
Rolls on her back and purrs like a cat
But at door-bell's ring hell's proverbial bat
With ear-splitting bark will terrorise
The unwelcome caller, then recognise
A fan of her own who comes every week
And fawning subside with a near-human shriek.

Then after a prowl in the garden dark
Tiger-eyes yellow in moonlight stark,
She'll share my biscuits, but that's not all
Now it's time for bed, she brings her ball!

THE BALLAD OF THE CATS

'Candy' we named our dear little tabby;
She'd been the victim of treatment shabby,
Though in a few weeks you scarce would guess
An abandoned waif once was this princess.

She had all the airs of a high-born Puss,
Despite her privations, fastidious,
Eyes pools of amber, dainty of paw,
A cute little face in a halo of fur.

She reigned as a queen until one day we moved,
An event of which she quite disapproved;
We hunted her everywhere, agonised,
Despairing, in newspaper advertised.

Then Tigger turned up, right out of the blue,
Took over the place as only he knew;
No beauty was he; a gregarious chap,
Brought in all his friends through Candy's cat-flap.

Till one day the phone rang; said a friendly voice:
'I think I've found Candy!' Did we rejoice!
She'd been living wild; now, with tigress-like ire,
The usurper she chased from her place by the fire.

Tigger sprang at his rival, bearing his claws,
Snatched a chunk of her fur with a snap of his jaws;
With frantic miaow Candy leapt on my knee,
Disdainfully snarled at such temerity.

The cat-flap crashed noisily: Tigger was gone,
Too proud to stay not to be Number One;
When out for a walk I met him one day,
He rubbed close against me and went on his way.

Tigger was a roamer, Tigger came to call,
He would settle on his terms, or not at all.

THE DOLPHIN'S LAMENT

Do you remember how in picture-books
The dolphins swam in rolling emerald seas,
With elfin children riding on their backs,
While distantly sails billowed in the breeze?

Bright jets of water flashed in diamond spray
On gleaming blue-black bodies leaping high
To startle laughing mermaids at their play,
Exultant silhouettes in summer sky.

Black shadows sinister now stain the swell
Where flounder dying birds with oil-clogged plumes;
Dead fish-shoals toss in oscillating hell
As breaker on the shore pollution spumes.

In mammoth net which trawls the ocean floor
My starving brother writhes with flippers snared,
While stricken cormorants the cruel mesh claw
And neither rarity nor beauty's spared.

Through swirling currents dark the spilt blood spreads,
Foul evidence of harpoon's deadly quest,
As tortured whales with entrails torn to shreds
From killer man last mortal combat wrest.

Where lethal cargo-ships churn sluggish seas
And once again the obscene hold is sprung,
The waters burn and spew new-born disease,
And sickly seals abort their malformed young.

Yet man unsated probes the watery deeps
And Neptune's ancient kingdom violates,
Unheeding still the ravished harvests reaps,
Our ocean habitation devastates.

Sealed is the spoiler's doom by his own hand;
Soon yields to fear that gleeful dominance:
When ice-cap thaw unleashed claims drowning land
Mermaids will play again and dolphins dance.

BATTERED WOMEN

You're smashing , my darling, with your eyes of clear blue;
Look deep into mine, dear; to you I'll be true!
He did not say then how his cruel fist would crack
The gleam from the sapphires, leave them swollen and black.

Your teeth are like pearls, kid, they flash in the sun;
Come, kiss me and win me; we two shall be one!
He did not say then, after some drunken bout
Her gums would be bleeding, teeth broken, knocked out.

Your hair is spun gold, luv, as light as the breeze;
To touch it is bliss, luv; be mine, mine to please!
He did not say then she would cower from this brute,
Her hair in his clawing pulled out to the root.

In tiny bikini she ran on the shore,
Her limbs lithe and shapely: What pins, he said; cor!
He did not say then he would throw her downstairs
And leave her a cripple; racked with pain, she despairs.

Your arms, they entwine me; I can't let you go!
Come, marry me, darling; my love you must know!
He did not say then to be crossed drove him wild;
Her arms now are broken. She can't hold her child.

How quickly your heart beats, my dearest, my own;
To you I'll be faithful, sweet girl, you alone!
He did not say then other hearts he had bled,
With blows had chastised them: Her heart failed. She's dead.

THE STONING

I mourn you, Arab sister, shed my tears
Over your broken body done to death
By punishment of primitive design.

My anger seethes that you, a tender girl
In your first bloom, were raped
By youths emboldened of forbidden drugs
Who you as temptress then denounced,
Themselves proclaiming innocent of guilt.

In cruel shackles you were brought to bear
Your child thus fathered wantonly,
- Poor female babe, what destiny is yours? -
Still weak from your ordeal were dragged
By hands of men, self-righteous hypocrites,
Your eyes dark mirrors of unfathomed dread,
To desert-place, submitted to the lashing law prescribed,
With filthy gag to stifle anguished cries.

Men gathered, scrabbling in the dust for rocks
To hurl in frenzied zeal at your poor frame;
I sense the thud, the sickening jerk
Of limbs with every nerve on fire,
Until, with all pulse fled,
Officious word pronounced you dead,

What law is this? What misinterpretation of divine intent
Ordains for women such barbarity
And yet absolves, save for some paltry admonition,
Its men from guilt? (Shades of Eve perhaps?)
How long before our sleeping Goddess wakes?
How long before the laws we must obey
Are women's laws by women freely made?

Based on a report in 'Amnesty'

ZANA

As women celebrate their onward march
And bask in new achievements' glittering rays
I would acclaim the triumph of a girl
Whose father saw her as a female pawn
To barter into foreign marriage bond.

Schooled in the knowledge of her equal worth
This heroine forgave not, nor forgot
That bass denial of her human rights.
And like a beacon through those nightmare years
That knowledge gleamed: I will go home, she said.

Living a half-life on the edge of hell
Raped, beaten, slave to her husband's family,
Bearing her child in unalleviated pain
Amidst the stench of dung, the filth, the flies,
Grinding with Dark Age tool the corn,
With body bent beneath the cruel abuse
Of long days spent in seeding arid soil,
Of humping water; still she moaned, I will go home
And brushed away the tears with dust-smeared hand.

Apprised in secret of her daughter's plight,
As outraged tigress claws the net that snares
Her helpless young, her mother tore
At the dissembling web of bureaucratic guile,
Enrolling allies, vowed: She shall come home.

And she came home: out of that darkness holding yet,
Captive of their children's love, her sister.
Then pause to honour this courageous feat:
Nor let the light-swathed pinnacles new-scaled
Dazzle your eyes to the shadowed vales below
Whence comes the countermarch of feared oppression.

STREETS

When you built your house next to mine
A street was born, so line on line
Through cities slicing, straight as arrow,
Carrying juggernauts, coster-barrow
In villages by pub and church
Twisting drunkenly, probe or lurch
A billion streets. And footsteps pound
The stony pavements, concrete-bound;
A street-world formed of mud and grit,
Of rutted cart-tracks, lantern-lit,
Where tarmac now smooths motor's way
And glistens black in street-lamp's ray.

She's lived for years in every street,
White-haired old lady on shuffling feet,
Fumbling across to number five
To see the old man's still alive
'And kicking yet!' 'And her at three?'
'Don't ask me, luv; she don't speak to me!'
The usual scene at number ten:
'How do they do it? A new car again!'
'Dawn raid? What's that? At twenty-four?'
'Stolen goods, drugs - God knows what more!'-

'So number thirty's up for sale?'
At number forty macho male
Has parked his lorry. 'It lowers the tone,'
Snorts social climber at forty-one.
Down at fifty the curtains drawn
Betoken death; the street will mourn.

This is the pattern; no man's an isle;
We live with each other, fret or smile,
Setting our dwellings side by side,
Moving down streets, a human tide,
Bent on survival, keep going or drop
In streets where we live, streets where we shop.

Streets made their mark in history,
In fiction too: turn on TV!
Watling Street by the Romans traced,
London burned when Pudding Lane blazed,
Baker Street, Sherlock Holmes' retreat,
Christmas shopping in Oxford Street:
A pageant of streets through time displayed,
Your house and mine in that cavalcade.

GOING COMPREHENSIVE IN 1967

Perhaps the ideal was right:
Multi-class, multi-ability, progressing together
Into a future bound to be bright.

Realities - bewildered identities
Housed in split-site conglomeration
Of clumsily linked and adapted buildings -
Fell short of our expectation.

Striving to reach Block B on time from Block A
Across the main road, some distance away,
We glimpsed the Headmaster, jealously watched
By down-graded rivals, playing tiddly-winks
On unworkable time-table, devised
By whizz-kid Co-ordinator while
Expounding on modules and schedules;
Ex-deputy Head, stripped of authority,
Shuffled, eyes glazed, in leaky old school
He once ran, through personal hell of humiliation.

Super-efficient former Head of the French Department
(Grammar School) after teaching the fifteenth stream,
Succumbed to hypertension,
And kindly, long-serving Home Ecs. Mrs. B.
Shook her head over boys rolling pastry.

'Old Baldie' took 4Y for 3D (marooned at the baths)
And taught them geography; they never asked
Why the 'Prof' wasn't there , teaching them history.
Probationer, writing 2C's reports,
Did 2G's by mistake, not even her class.

Singing ' Past three o'clock' on the last afternoon
Summed up all our frustration; so ended
The first term of comprehensivisation.

DOWNBEAT

So, still at the wicket, one has reached
The half-century. There comes
No acknowledging cheer from the crowd,
Only the onrush of panic
At the unavoidable, mediocre slotting
Into history, identity lost,
And the questioning of the validity
Of one's very existence:
The failure to make by one's presence
The indelible mark.

And one stumbles on, conscience murmuring,
Through the corridor maze of life's museum,
Magically, electronically, touching off
The illumination of memories
Without connection:
The tantrum over a sibling's toy,
Hasty words spoken, too late regretted,
A door slammed, an ornament broken,
Tears shed amidst wind-tossed daffodils,
Betokening love, grief and guilt.

Strange, that scenes of success and elation
Are blurred, that a life-time's vocation
Seems without worth,
Tapering into a void, the here and now
An aching confusion:
Life soon over, or just beginning, beckoning
To new aspiration,
Before the final march
To the pavilion.

THE ENIGMA OF BEAUTY

Beauty: the very word stirs on the air
As haunting oboe strain, elusive, rare,
For you may beauty find, or hear, or see
In spheres of bleak indifference to me,
And where blind rancour, spite to our hearts cleave
Then will they beauty's presence scarce perceive;
Anger distorts the sunset gleam of snow,
The ribboned hues of newly-arched rainbow;
The fairest rose its bloom unmarked displays
If avarice and greed our visions haze.

Yet where there's pain or sorrow, doubt, distress,
The misting eye will clear, grief find redress
In bluebell vistas, glades of beechen green,
Pure melody which soars to vaults unseen,
Fragrance of summer flowers in grey twilight
Or nightingale's first song at fall of night.

Who then may beauty's tenuous bounds ordain,
Discern its mark in fragile porcelain,
Bright-painted barge on murky town canal,
In scent of jasmine, fine-toned madrigal?
I watched a lone tree's greening fronds windswept
In dingy street-lamp's beam, and could have wept,
Yet looked on fair art treasures quite unmoved
When crowded galleries constraining proved;
Beauty will not attend at our behest
But steals about the world in silent quest,
For Beauty is not easily defined;
Its precepts are redrawn within the mind.